Landform Top Tens

The World's Most Amazing Lakes

Michael Hurley

Chicago, Illinois

www.heinemannraintree.com
Visit our website to find out more information about Heinemann-Raintree books.

To order:
☎ Phone 888-454-2279
▣ Visit www.heinemannraintree.com to browse our catalog and order online.

© 2009 Raintree
an imprint of Capstone Global Library, LLC
Chicago, Illinois

Customer Service: 888-454-2279

Visit our website at www.heinemannraintree.com

Edited by Louise Galpine, Kate DeVilliers, and Rachel Howells
Designed by Victoria Bevan and Geoff Ward
Original illustrations © Capstone Global Library Limited
Illustrated by Geoff Ward
Picture research by Hannah Taylor
Production by Alison Parsons

Printed and bound in China by CTPS

13 12 11 10 09
10 9 8 7 6 5 4 3 2 1

Library of Congress Cataloging-in-Publication Data

Hurley, Michael, 1979-
  The world's most amazing lakes / Michael Hurley.
    p. cm. -- (Landform top tens)
  Includes bibliographical references and index.
  ISBN 978-1-4109-3703-2 (hc) -- ISBN 978-1-4109-3711-7 (pb)
  1. Lakes--Juvenile literature. I. Title.
  GB1603.8.H87 2008
  551.48'2--dc22
                          2008051532

Acknowledgments

We would like to thank the following for permission to reproduce photographs: Alamy p. **17** (Eugenio Opitz); Ardea.com p. **19** (Jean-Paul Ferrero); Corbis p. **16** (Paulo Fridman); Eye Ubiquitous/ Hutchison p. **12** (Victoria Ivlevla-Yorke); FLPA pp. **6** and **7** (Minden Pictures/ Konrad Wothe), **8** (Minden Pictures/ Jim Brandenburg), **20–21** (imagebroker / Guenter Fischer); istockphoto p. **25** (Anatoly Ustinenko); Lonely Planet pp. **15** (Dave Lewis), **18** (David Wall); naturepl p. **27** (Cameron Hansen); Photolibrary pp. **4–5** (Flirt Collection/ Bill Ross), **9** (F1 Online/ Acfotodesign), **10** (DEA/ M Borchi), **11** (Glow Images), **13** (JTB Photo), **14** (David Messent), **23** (OSF/ Mark Deeble and Victoria Stone), **26** (Imagestate/ Gavin Hellier); Still Pictures pp. **22** (McPHOTOs), **24** (Das Fotarchiv/ Knut Mueller).

Background images by Photodisc.

Cover photograph of Morn Harbor on the North coast of Lake Superior, reproduced with permission of Photolibrary (Radius Images).

We would like to thank Nick Lapthorn for his invaluable help in the preparation of this book.

Every effort has been made to contact copyright holders of material reproduced in this book. Any omissions will be rectified in subsequent printings if notice is given to the publishers.

Disclaimer

Contents

Some words are printed in bold, **like this**. You can find out what they mean by looking in the glossary on page 31.

Lakes

Lakes are large bodies of water that are found inland. The water in a lake never flows directly into the sea. Their water comes from rain, streams, and rivers. There are two different types of lake: saltwater and freshwater lakes. Lakes can be found all over the world, on every **continent**.

Crater Lake, in Oregon, formed in the crater of an extinct (inactive) volcano.

How lakes form

Lakes have formed in many different ways. Some of the world's lakes were created by melting **glaciers**. Other lakes have formed in **rift valleys**. A rift valley is created when Earth's **tectonic plates** are forced apart. This leaves a crack in Earth's surface. Over many years this crack fills with water, creating a lake. Sometimes lakes form in the **craters** of **extinct volcanoes**. Humans can also create lakes, when we build dams to block the flow of rivers.

Limnology

Limnology is the name given to the study of lakes. Someone who studies lakes is known as a limnologist.

Lake Baikal

Lake Baikal in Russia is the oldest and deepest lake in the world. It was formed in a **rift valley** over 25 million years ago. More than 350 rivers flow into Lake Baikal, which plunges to a depth of 1,620 meters (5,315 feet). This ancient lake is a freshwater lake, and it is thought to be one of the cleanest lakes in the world. Its waters are so clean that some is used as bottled drinking water.

The rocky beaches at the edge of Lake Baikal are unspoiled. This is because the lake is a protected World Heritage Site.

Omul salmon

Tourism and fishing are very important for the people who live near Lake Baikal. The local **economy** depends on there being enough Omul salmon in the lake for people to fish. This fish is a **delicacy** and is found nowhere else in the world.

The beautiful Baikal seal can only be found in the wild at Lake Baikal.

LAKE BAIKAL

LOCATION:
RUSSIA, ASIA

DEPTH:
1,620 METERS
(5,315 FEET)

VOLUME:
23,000 KM³
(5,518 CUBIC MILES)

TYPE:
FRESH WATER

THAT'S AMAZING!
LAKE BAIKAL CONTAINS
20 PERCENT OF THE WORLD'S
TOTAL UNFROZEN
FRESHWATER RESERVES.

Lake Baikal

ASIA

Pacific
Ocean

Indian
Ocean

Amazing wildlife

Because of its age and location, Lake Baikal has an amazing variety of plants and animals. Some of these plants and animals are not found anywhere else in the world. This lake is a **UNESCO** World Heritage Site because it contains wildlife that is important to all of the world's people.

Lake Superior

Lake Superior is the largest, deepest, and coldest of North America's Great Lakes. The Great Lakes are a collection of five lakes that lay on the border between North America and Canada. Lake Superior measures 405 meters (1,329 feet) at its deepest point.

Lake Superior has carved out some amazing rocky scenery at its shores.

LAKE SUPERIOR

LOCATION:
UNITED STATES AND CANADA, NORTH AMERICA

DEPTH:
UP TO 405 METERS (1,329 FEET)

VOLUME:
12,100 KM³ (2,903 CUBIC MILES)

TYPE:
FRESH WATER

THAT'S AMAZING!
LAKE SUPERIOR IS THE LARGEST FRESHWATER LAKE IN THE WORLD.

NORTH AMERICA

Lake Superior

Pacific Ocean

Atlantic Ocean

Large waves can be seen on Lake Superior. Strong winds whip up the waters, and waves over 9 meters (30 feet) have been recorded!

Isle Royale

Lake Superior has an island in it that is a national park. This island is called Isle Royale. There are smaller lakes on Isle Royale that also have islands! These lakes and islands are not very big compared to the enormous Lake Superior.

Lake Titicaca

Lake Titicaca is one of the world's highest lakes. It is 3,810 meters (12,500 feet) above sea level. The lake is in the Andes mountain range, and it stretches across two countries, Peru and Bolivia. It is both the largest lake by **volume** and the largest freshwater lake in South America. Five major rivers flow into the lake, bringing **meltwater** down from **glaciers** on the surrounding mountains.

Lake Titicaca is over three million years old. **Archaeologists** have found remains there that date back thousands of years.

LAKE TITICACA

LOCATION:
PERU AND BOLIVIA, SOUTH AMERICA

DEPTH:
UP TO 300 METERS (984 FEET)

VOLUME:
AROUND 800 KM³ (192 CUBIC MILES)

TYPE:
FRESH WATER

THAT'S AMAZING!
THE AIR TEMPERATURE AROUND LAKE TITICACA CAN GO FROM -10°C (14°F) IN WINTER TO 23°C (73°F) IN THE SUMMER.

SOUTH AMERICA

Pacific Ocean

Atlantic Ocean

Lake Titicaca

Floating islands

On the western side of Lake Titicaca there are about 70 small islands that float. They have been made by the Uros people. Floating roots are clumped together and covered with a large amount of cut reeds. Small huts have been built on the islands. The islands are strong enough to float even with humans living on them. They are an amazing sight!

These human-made islands on Lake Titicaca support people and their homes.

Aral Sea

The Aral Sea is a lake. It is called a sea because it was once part of a much larger body of water. The Aral Sea is thought to be over five million years old, and it used to be the world's fourth-largest lake. However, it is now mostly desert. In the 1960s, rivers in the area were **diverted** from flowing into the Aral Sea. The rivers were diverted to fields because water was needed to grow cotton. Within 20 years the Aral Sea had halved in size. Today, the Aral Sea has lost 90 percent of the water that used to flow into it, and the lake is now only one-third of its original size.

The Aral Sea is in danger of drying up completely.

ARAL SEA

LOCATION:
UZBEKISTAN AND
KAZAKHSTAN, ASIA

DEPTH:
40.4 METERS (133 FEET)

VOLUME:
193 KM^3
(46 CUBIC MILES)

TYPE:
SALT WATER

THAT'S AMAZING!
SCIENTISTS BELIEVE THAT, UNLESS
ACTION IS TAKEN SOON, THE
ARAL SEA WILL BE A COMPLETE
DESERT WITHIN 20 TO 30 YEARS.

ASIA

Aral Sea

Indian
Ocean

This "graveyard" ship has been left to rust in the empty Aral Sea.

Toxic dust storms

As the Aral Sea has dried out, it has left behind huge areas of
dusty, salty land. This land is full of chemicals that have been
used in the cotton industry. When the wind blows in these
areas, it carries toxic dust to other regions. This toxic
dust is very dangerous to humans and animals.

Lake Victoria

The largest freshwater lake in Africa is Lake Victoria. It is the second-largest freshwater lake in the world. The lake is so large that it covers parts of three countries: Tanzania, Kenya, and Uganda. The location of the lake makes it a very important transportation link for the people who live in these countries.

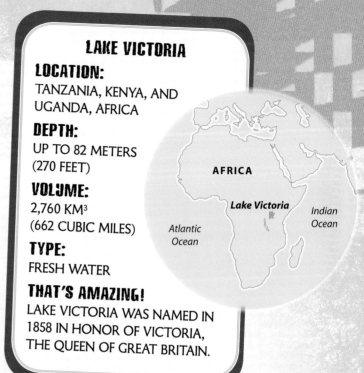

LAKE VICTORIA

LOCATION:
TANZANIA, KENYA, AND UGANDA, AFRICA

DEPTH:
UP TO 82 METERS (270 FEET)

VOLUME:
2,760 KM³ (662 CUBIC MILES)

TYPE:
FRESH WATER

THAT'S AMAZING!
LAKE VICTORIA WAS NAMED IN 1858 IN HONOR OF VICTORIA, THE QUEEN OF GREAT BRITAIN.

AFRICA

Atlantic Ocean

Lake Victoria

Indian Ocean

Fishing boats on Lake Victoria help local people make a living.

The Luo people live in this fishing village on the shores of Lake Victoria.

The Luo people

Many people live around Lake Victoria. The Luo people settled there more than 500 years ago. The lake provided good land for cattle to feed on, and the lake itself had many fish. Natural building materials such as clay and strong reeds were used to make homes. Many Luo people still rely on the lake's natural environment for their work and shelter.

Lake Maracaibo

Lake Maracaibo is the largest lake in South America. It is in Venezuela, in the north of the **continent**. Lake Maracaibo lies in the extremely hot, humid lowlands of the Maracaibo **basin**. The Maracaibo basin area contains 25 percent of Venezuela's population. The lake includes the largest oil fields in South America. Oil is removed from the lake and made into **petroleum**.

Lake Maracaibo is the center of Venezuela's oil industry. Here are some of its oil wells.

LAKE MARACAIBO

LOCATION:
VENEZUELA, SOUTH AMERICA

DEPTH:
UP TO 50 METERS (165 FEET)

VOLUME:
280 KM^3 (67 CUBIC MILES)

TYPE:
PART FRESH WATER,
PART **BRACKISH**

THAT'S AMAZING!
THE LAKE COVERS AN AREA OF 13,280 KM^2 (5,130 SQ MILES)—THAT IS JUST SLIGHTLY SMALLER THAN CONNECTICUT!

Lake Maracaibo

Pacific
Ocean

SOUTH AMERICA

Atlantic
Ocean

Polluted fish

Petroleum is the most important local industry in Venezuela. Sugarcane and cacao are grown in this area, and livestock are also raised. Another very important industry is fishing. Thousands of people rely on the lake's supply of fish. Unfortunately, the fish in the lake have been affected by **pollution** from farm chemicals and oil spills.

Amazing bridge

Connecting the shore on either side of Lake Maracaibo is one of the longest bridges in the world. The General Rafael Urdaneta Bridge is 8.7 km (5.4 miles) long. It is located at the narrowest point of the lake.

Lake Eyre

The largest lake in **Australasia** is Lake Eyre in Australia. Amazingly, the lake is often dry. There is very little rainfall in the area, so the lake fills up just twice every 100 years. If the lake fills with water completely, it then takes two years to dry up again. The rivers that flow into the lake are severely affected by **evaporation**. Temperatures are so high that the water in the rivers dries up before it reaches the lake.

This photo shows the waters of Lake Eyre slowly drying up.

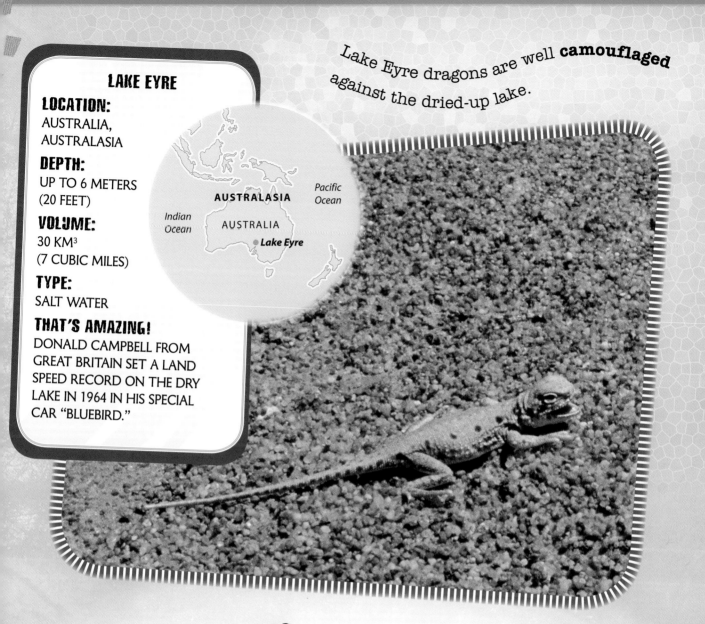

Lake Eyre dragons are well **camouflaged** against the dried-up lake.

LAKE EYRE

LOCATION:
AUSTRALIA,
AUSTRALASIA

DEPTH:
UP TO 6 METERS
(20 FEET)

VOLUME:
30 KM³
(7 CUBIC MILES)

TYPE:
SALT WATER

THAT'S AMAZING!
DONALD CAMPBELL FROM
GREAT BRITAIN SET A LAND
SPEED RECORD ON THE DRY
LAKE IN 1964 IN HIS SPECIAL
CAR "BLUEBIRD."

AUSTRALASIA

Pacific
Ocean

Indian
Ocean

AUSTRALIA

● Lake Eyre

Lake Eyre dragons

The **ecosystem** of Lake Eyre has some amazing animals.
One of these animals is called the Lake Eyre dragon. It
is a small lizard. These lizards survive by eating ants and
other insects. It is so hot in this region that the Lake Eyre
dragons try to move as quickly as possible. They also
have spiky scales around their eyes. These scales protect
them from the glare of the sun.

Lake Geneva

Lake Geneva is very famous because of its natural beauty. The lake is in Europe and lies between France and Switzerland. Lake Geneva is the largest freshwater lake in Western Europe. It covers 548 km² (212 sq miles) and can reach depths of 310 meters (1,017 feet). The water in Lake Geneva is unusually blue and **transparent**. The level of the water can change quickly. This is because of seiches. Seiches are changes in the level of the water in the lake due to wind and waves.

Rich and famous

Lake Geneva is very popular with tourists all year round. The amazing scenery around the lake includes mountains, castles, and small villages. There are also many houses on the shore of the lake itself. Rich and famous people, such as movie stars and musicians, own some of these houses. The restaurants on the shores of the lake sell fish that are caught on the lake.

Lake Geneva and the surrounding area is one of the most beautiful places in the world.

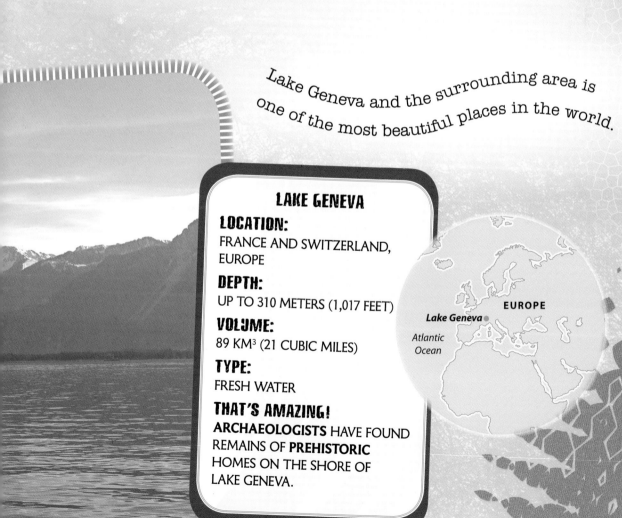

LAKE GENEVA

LOCATION:
FRANCE AND SWITZERLAND, EUROPE

DEPTH:
UP TO 310 METERS (1,017 FEET)

VOLUME:
89 KM³ (21 CUBIC MILES)

TYPE:
FRESH WATER

THAT'S AMAZING!
ARCHAEOLOGISTS HAVE FOUND REMAINS OF **PREHISTORIC** HOMES ON THE SHORE OF LAKE GENEVA.

EUROPE

Lake Geneva

Atlantic Ocean

Lake Tanganyika

Lake Tanganyika is in Africa. It is a freshwater lake and is the deepest lake on the **continent**. Lake Tanganyika is the third-largest lake in the world by **volume**. The lake is so large that it covers parts of four countries: Burundi, Democratic Republic of Congo, Tanzania, and Zambia. Lake Tanganyika is an important transportation and communications link between these countries. Almost one million people live near the lake.

People use boats to get across Lake Tanganyika.

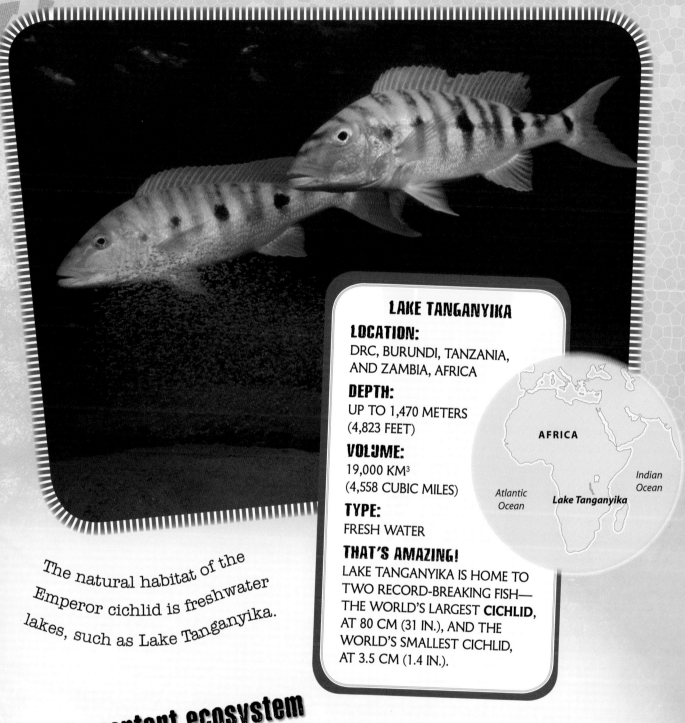

The natural habitat of the Emperor cichlid is freshwater lakes, such as Lake Tanganyika.

LAKE TANGANYIKA

LOCATION:
DRC, BURUNDI, TANZANIA, AND ZAMBIA, AFRICA

DEPTH:
UP TO 1,470 METERS (4,823 FEET)

VOLUME:
19,000 KM³ (4,558 CUBIC MILES)

TYPE:
FRESH WATER

THAT'S AMAZING!
LAKE TANGANYIKA IS HOME TO TWO RECORD-BREAKING FISH—THE WORLD'S LARGEST **CICHLID**, AT 80 CM (31 IN.), AND THE WORLD'S SMALLEST CICHLID, AT 3.5 CM (1.4 IN.).

AFRICA

Atlantic Ocean

Lake Tanganyika

Indian Ocean

Important ecosystem

Lake Tanganyika is one of the most important **ecosystems** in the world. The lake's ecosystem contains more than 2,000 plant and animal **species**. Around 600 of these species do not exist anywhere else in the world.

Caspian Sea

The Caspian Sea is the largest lake in the world by **volume**. It is the largest and deepest saltwater lake in the world. Historically, this lake was thought to be a sea because of its size. It is known as a terminal lake. This means that its water does not flow into an ocean. The Caspian Sea has many **tributaries** flowing into it from the north. Over 130 rivers flow into it, including the Volga and the Ural.

During the summer months, the shores of the Caspian Sea look beautiful.

CASPIAN SEA

LOCATION:
IRAN, AZERBAIJAN, RUSSIA, KAZAKHSTAN, AND TURKMENISTAN, ASIA

DEPTH:
UP TO 1,025 METERS (3,363 FEET)

VOLUME:
78,000 KM³ (18,713 CUBIC MILES)

TYPE:
SALT WATER

THAT'S AMAZING!
ABOUT 90 PERCENT OF ALL THE WORLD'S STURGEONS (A TYPE OF FISH) ARE FOUND IN THE CASPIAN SEA. THERE ARE SEVEN **SPECIES** OF STURGEON IN THE LAKE.

ASIA

Caspian Sea

Indian Ocean

Thick ice walls form at the edges of the Caspian Sea during the winter.

Frozen edges

During winter months the temperature around the Caspian Sea can fall below -20°C (-4°F). This means that ice that is many feet thick forms at the northern parts of the lake.

Lakes in Danger

Lakes are very important to humans. Not only are they beautiful places to visit and explore, but they can also be important sources of drinking water and food. Their waters are often used in farming and for fishing, and many people rely on lakes to make a living. Animals and plants also rely on lakes—and some types of wildlife live only in one particular lake!

If lakes get polluted, causing fish to die, fishermen and their families will suffer.

An oil spill has polluted the waters of this lake in Thailand.

Unfortunately, human activities, such as the use of chemicals in farming, have led to the **pollution** of lakes. When lakes become polluted, their waters are not safe to drink, and fish and other animals can be seriously harmed. In some cases the use of water from lakes for farming has caused the lakes to dry up almost completely. This has devastating effects for the whole **ecosystem**.

In many countries, governments create national parks to protect lakes and their surrounding areas. This means that the beautiful scenery, animals, and plants will be there for us all to enjoy for many years to come.

Lake Facts and Figures

There are lakes all over the world, of all different shapes and sizes. Some lakes were created by the shifting of Earth's **tectonic plates,** and some are human-made. Some are millions of years old. Which lake do you think is the most amazing?

This map of the world shows all the lakes described in this book.

Arctic Ocean

NORTH AMERICA

Lake Superior

Atlantic Ocean

Lake Maracaibo

SOUTH AMERICA

Lake Titicaca

Pacific Ocean

EUROPE

Lake Geneva

AFRICA

Lake Victoria

Lake Tanganyika

ASIA

Lake Baikal

Aral Sea

CaspianSea

Indian Ocean

Pacific Ocean

AUSTRALASIA

Lake Eyre

Southern Ocean

ANTARCTICA

LAKE BAIKAL

DEPTH:
1,620 METERS
(5,315 FEET)

VOLUME:
23,000 KM³
(5,518 CUBIC MILES)

TYPE:
FRESH WATER

LAKE SUPERIOR

DEPTH:
UP TO 405 METERS
(1,329 FEET)

VOLUME:
12,100 KM³
(2,903 CUBIC MILES)

TYPE:
FRESH WATER

LAKE TITICACA

DEPTH:
UP TO 300 METERS
(984 FEET)

VOLUME:
AROUND 800 KM³
(192 CUBIC MILES)

TYPE:
FRESH WATER

ARAL SEA

DEPTH:
40.4 METERS (133 FEET)

VOLUME:
193 KM³
(46 CUBIC MILES)

TYPE:
SALT WATER

LAKE VICTORIA

DEPTH:
UP TO 82 METERS
(270 FEET)

VOLUME:
2,760 KM³
(662 CUBIC MILES)

TYPE:
FRESH WATER

LAKE MARACAIBO

DEPTH:
UP TO 50 METERS
(165 FEET)

VOLUME:
280 KM³
(67 CUBIC MILES)

TYPE:
PART FRESH WATER,
PART **BRACKISH**

LAKE EYRE

DEPTH:
UP TO 6 METERS
(20 FEET)

VOLUME:
30 KM³
(7 CUBIC MILES)

TYPE:
SALT WATER

LAKE GENEVA

DEPTH:
UP TO 310 METERS
(1,017 FEET)

VOLUME:
89 KM³
(21 CUBIC MILES)

TYPE:
FRESH WATER

LAKE TANGANYIKA

DEPTH:
UP TO 1,470 METERS
(4,823 FEET)

VOLUME:
19,000 KM³
(4,558 CUBIC MILES)

TYPE:
FRESH WATER

CASPIAN SEA

DEPTH:
UP TO 1,025 METERS
(3,363 FEET)

VOLUME:
78,000 KM³
(18,713 CUBIC MILES)

TYPE:
SALT WATER

Find Out More

Books to read

Braun, Eric, and Sandra Donovan. *Biomes: Rivers, Lakes, and Ponds.*
Chicago: Raintree, 2002.

Chambers, Catherine, and Nicholas Lapthorn. *Mapping Earthforms:
Lakes.* Chicago: Heinemann Library, 2008.

Holland, Simon. *DK Eye Wonder: Rivers and Lakes.*
New York: Dorling Kindersley, 2003.

Websites

National Geographic
www.nationalgeographic.org
Use this website to search for lakes and to find out more
about the wildlife that lives in and around them.

The International Lake Environment Committee
www.ilec.or.jp
This website has a huge database with information
about all of the world's lakes.

LakeNet
www.worldlakes.org
Find out more about the lakes of the world. You
can also take a look at the lake gallery of photographs
and images.

Glossary

archaeologist someone who studies human history by digging up and studying ancient remains

Australasia term used to describe Australia, New Zealand, and a series of nearby islands in the Pacific Ocean

basin lake floor that slopes downward

brackish salty, but not salty enough to be saltwater

camouflage skin color or pattern that disguises an animal against its background

cichlid freshwater fish

continent continuous landmass

crater bowl-shaped opening at the top of a volcano

delicacy delicious food

divert change direction

economy money coming in and out of a country or area

ecosystem community of living things and the place they live in

evaporation when heat changes a liquid into vapor (steam)

extinct volcano volcano that has not erupted for millions of years

glacier river of ice that flows slowly down a mountain

meltwater water that has melted from ice and snow

petroleum liquid mixture that can be extracted from underground and made into fuel

pollution waste and dirt that can damage Earth

prehistoric something that is from a time before history was first recorded

rift valley steep-sided valley created when two tectonic plates are pushed apart

species particular type of living thing

tectonic plate huge piece of Earth's crust

transparent something that is clear enough to see through

tributary small river that flows into another bigger river or lake

UNESCO United Nations Educational, Scientific, and Cultural Organization

volume amount of space that a liquid or object takes up

Index

4/10